Lucien Bély

Wonderful
MONT SAINT-MICHEL

Photographs by Hervé Champollion
Translated by Paul Williams
and Angela Moyon

EDITIONS OUEST-FRANCE
13, rue du Breil, Rennes

By the same author for
Editions Ouest-France

Wonderful Camargue and Les-Saintes Maries-de-la-Mer (available in French, German and italian)
Wonderful Normandy : co-author M.B. Baranger (available in French, German, English, Italian and Spanish)
A Guide to Normandy (available in French and English)
A History of France (available in French and English)
A History of Mont Saint-Michel (available in French, German, and English)
Louis XIV
Le Mont Saint-Michel, monastère et citadelle
Mont Saint-Michel (available in French, German, English, Dutch, Italian, and Spanish)
Normandy (available in French, German, English, and Italian)
Les Baux de Provence (available in French and German)
Fontaine-de-Vaucluse (available in French, German, and English)
Les Saintes-Maries-de-la-Mer (available in French and German)

Above : *the salt marshes.*

Middle : *the Knights' Chamber.*

Opposite : *Mont Saint-Michel by night.*

Right : *Mont Saint-Michel seen from the west.*

Front cover : *an aerial view of Mont Saint-Michel.*

Back cover : *Michael, the archangel.*

THE HISTORY OF MONT SAINT-MICHEL

The story of the rock, the forest and the sea

Try to imagine the Mont Saint-Michel before anything was built on it. It was a two hundred and fifty foot high rock with sheer sides. The granite which it is made up of, is a very hard rock which, for thousands of years, has resisted erosion from wind and water. This is the reason why this rock, together with one or two others, stands out in what is generally low-lying country.

Around the rock was forest, which may have been called Scissy Forest. It has now disappeared, for the sea over the years engulfed it. Some tree trunks have actually been found buried in the sand. According to legend, an enormous tidal wave swept over the area, transforming it completely at the beginning of the 8th century when Bishop Aubert dedicated the rock to Saint Michael. Ever since then, it has been an island just like the rock next to it, which is known as Tombelaine.

The tide in the bay where the rock stands, is among the strongest in the world. The difference in depth of water between low and high tide in the same place is around forty feet. The beaches are almost completely flat. The sea has to come in many miles in just a few hours before reaching high water mark. The sea comes in at an amazing speed. It can be as fast as a horse at the gallop, and can prove quite dangerous for people fishing or walking on the beach.

Three rivers flow out onto the shore : the Sée, the Sélune and the Couesnon. The latter marks the boundary between Brittany and Normandy, for as the old

Mont Saint-Michel seen from the north-east.

They swept aside Roman gods and the ancient gods who inhabited woods and pools of water. To escape from the company of their fellow men and from worldly pleasures, holy men, called hermits, lived in great poverty in lonely forests and deserted islands. The place which we now call Mont Saint-Michel was known in those days as Mont Tombe which meant literally « tomb on a hill ». The rock no doubt attracted hermits, for Christians, perhaps from Ireland, had settled very early on around the bay and near Dol-de-Bretagne. A remarkable legend tells us how fishermen provided food for the hermits living on the Mont. Whenever a hermit went hungry, he lit a fire ; the villagers saw the smoke and loaded up a donkey with provisions. God then guided it through what remained of the Forest of Scissy until it arrived safely at the holy man's refuge. One day a wolf devoured the innocent donkey and, as a punishment, God forced it to carry all the provisions from then on.

Mont Saint-Michel seen from the south.

saying gœs : « The Couesnon's act of folly left the Mont in Normandy ». The grey silt, known locally as « tangue », gives delicate colouring to the landscape. Grass grows on those areas of the sandy shore which are no longer covered at high tide. The sheep that graze there are known locally as « pré-salés » (salt-meadow) sheep because of the salty tang in the grass.

In this land of sand, sky and sea was built an abbey in the style of a citadel, the overall height of which, including the church's steeple, is well over five hundred feet.

The hermits

As the Roman Empire declined, a new religion appeared : Christianity. Men who believed in one God and in his son, Jesus of Nazareth, were overrunning Europe.

Barnacle geese in the bay.

Meanwhile, the cult of Saint Michael was spreading from the East towards Gaul. Heavenly beings were the angels and the archangels Michael, Raphael and Gabriel. According to the Bible, when Lucifer, the fallen angel, compared himself with God, another angel stood up before him and shouted « Who is like God ? », in other words Mi-ka-el, or Michael. God entrusted him to lead his army, for Michael is « Prince of the Heavenly Host ». He wears a suit of armour or a long white tunic. He holds a sparkling sword or lance. In the Apocalypse, a book written by the Apostle, Saint John, a dragon with seven crowned heads and horns, and a tail that swept aside the stars, threatened the Virgin Mary and her Holy Child who had just been born. Michael and his angels fought this serpent from Satan and destroyed it.

Aubert dedicates the rock to Saint Michael

The Archangel often appeared in Italy : in Rome near the castle which still bears the name Holy Angel, and at Monte Gargano, a rocky peninsular on the Adriatic Sea.

The town of Avranches, which is very close to the Mont, in the year 708 was ruled by a bishop called Aubert. One night, he saw Saint Michael in a dream. The archangel ordered him to make the rock that had just been surrounded by the sea, into a place of worship dedicated to him. Aubert did nothing about it, thinking his imagination had got the better of him. Saint Michael grew impatient with him, and when he appeared the

third time, he poked a hole in Aubert's skull to make him believe. He caused many more miracles to take place, so as to convince the bishop and his followers. A bull that had been stolen, was found at the very top of the Mont, as Michael had predicted. One story has it that Aubert was to build his church as large as the area trodden on by the bull ; according to another story, it was to occupy the space left dry in the midst of the morning dew.

Aubert fulfilled Michael's wishes and despatched messengers to Monte Gargano in Italy. They bought back some sacred relics : a piece of the red cloak worn by the Archangel during one of his apparitions, and a fragment of the altar where he had placed his foot.

When they returned, Aubert began to construct the sanctuary. The builders received some divine assistance with their task. An old man who lived nearby was called by God to move a huge stone. Another story tells of how a small child simply touched it with his foot and pushed it over the edge. There was no drinking water on the rock, but miraculously a spring was discovered. This is now called Saint Aubert's spring.

As time went by, the rock began to be known as Mont Saint-Michel, and Aubert sent a few men to live there and pray to God and his Archangel.

The foundation of the abbey

The peace and prosperity brought by Charlemagne lasted a short while. Men from the North, or Normans, came and pillaged the coast every year. Their fast, slen-

The abbey seen from the south-east.

The abbey seen from the south-west.

from Flanders guided by a man of noble family called Maynard. These eleven monks adopted the rule of Saint Benedict which required them to organise their lives according to the principles of poverty, chastity and obedience. The abbey had become a Benedictine abbey.

The monk's leader was the abbot, or « father » of the community. He administered all the possessions of the monastery, encouraged the cult of Saint Michael, and received visitors. Theoretically, the monks themselves elected their own superior, but in practice, the Duke of Normandy, as protector of the abbey, persisted in selecting his own candidate for a long time.

The Romanesque age

The monk's vocation was to pray, both for themselves and for all men. Behind the high walls of the monastery, in the « enclosure », they avoided, as far as they could, all worldly temptations and violence. Their day was divided into eight hours : Matins at daybreak, Lauds, Prime, Terce, Sext around midday, Nones, Vespers, and Compline at the end of the day. Each of these hours was accompanied by prayers which were read out of « books of hours », or breviaries.

Knights, in feudal times, engaged themselves in the profession of arms. But as death grew near, they turned to the abbeys. A captain, Néel de Saint-Sauveur, sought refuge and peace on the Mont Saint-Michel. Many war-

der boats, known as drakkars, brought widespread terror. Above all else, they pillaged sanctuaries where there were objects of gold for the glory of God. The Mont had its fair share of these dreadful expeditions. In the end, the Normans came and settled, and the king of the Franks recognised one of their chiefs, Rolf le Marcheur, or Rollon, as the « Duke of Normandy ». In exchange, the formidable warrior became a Christian along with all his soldiers, and from then on protected all those in God's service.

Rollon and his descendants encouraged the rebuilding of important sanctuaries. But these new converts to the faith had high standards. Duke Richard reproached the priests who lived on the Mont for their immoral and impious behaviour. He threw them out and replaced them in 966 with submissive and humble monks

An aerial view of Mont Saint-Michel.

riors too asked to be buried in holy ground near sanctuaries.

When the old buildings were no longer big enough, the abbey, because of its wealth, was able to expand. An immense church was built at the top of the rock, to serve as a grandiose setting for prayer. Building techniques had progressed in Normandy. The style of architecture that later came to be known as Romanesque, was at its height. With the help of strong supporting pillars and huge arches to support beams and domes, the walls could be built extremely high. Two high towers, now no longer there, used to set off the façade of the church. To support this church, crypts, or subterranean chapels, were built along the contours of the rock. Their vaults, such as the one in the Saint-Martin crypt, were works of art. The very weight of the stones and the ingenious stonework ensured that the building was sound. The monks liked to pray in the half-light of the crypts. The living quarters, known as the «conventuels», occupied three floors in the northern part of the abbey. The dormitory (now the sacristy) was near the church ; below was the monks' promenade that has often been transformed over the ages ; finally, near the north-west door, was the so-called Aquilon room, built in the Romanesque style, where pilgrims were received.

Famous pilgrims

Very soon, famous pilgrims came to the Mont Saint-Michel to implore the Archangel's protection. Richard II, Duke of Normandy, married Judith of Brittany there in the presence of the nobility of both provinces. On that occasion, he offered the abbey some churches, mills, lands and forests. One Duke of Brittany placed on the altar, property deeds of lands which he was making over to the monastery. These numerous gifts amounted to a vast amount of property all around the Bay. Peasants, that worked on these lands, regularly transported to the island, either by boat or on carts at low tide, part of their harvests. In exchange they received protection and justice.

The abbot, in his turn, honoured the protectors of the abbey. When Duke William completed the conquest of England, the superior of the Mont sent six ships and four monks to salute the new king. The finest of all the abbots was Robert de Thorigny who had been a skilful member of the Court of the Plantagenet King, Henry II, who reigned over England and a large part of France. This abbot administered the abbey at the peak of its fortune. He welcomed there a whole line of magnificent princes. King Henry II, whom he served as counsellor,

came and visited him, accompanied by King Louis VII of France, the Archbishop of Rouen, two cardinals who later became Popes, and five abbots. Their entrance into the abbey was an occasion for sumptuous ceremony. The entire community awaited the royal visitors on the shore at the entrance to the town with the Gospels, incense and holy water. All the bells rang out as the distinguished gathering made for the church.

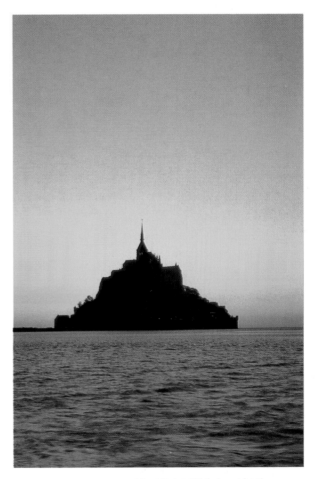

Mont Saint-Michel amidst the waves.

Overleaf : *Mont Saint-Michel and Tombelaine, islands in the bay.*

Robert de Thorigny added to the community by recruiting a larger number of monks during his travels ; he enriched the library, and finally had built, on the south-west side of the abbey, a huge hostel for pilgrims, which collapsed at the biginning of the 19th century. One the west side, he built his own quarters.

Mont Saint-Michel seen from the shore to the north-east.

The miracles

Whenever some strange, fortuitous event occurred on the Mont, it was always attributed to the influence of Saint Michael. The monks built up a whole collection of these « miracles » which pilgrims and travellers passed down over the centuries.

One day, a blind woman stood in front of the Mont, and when her face turned towards it, she recovered her sight. « How beautiful it is to be able to see », she exclaimed and the name Beauvoir (beautiful to see) was given to the village where she was. Another woman, who was expecting a child, unwisely attempted to cross the shore. She suddenly felt the first birth pangs and fell to the sand. The tide was coming in, but a miracle took place and she was spared. When the fishermen found her safe and sound, her child had been born.

The men of the Middle Ages thought that the bones of saints had miraculous powers. The bones of Bishop Aubert, now Saint Aubert, had disappeared. A long time after the foundation of the abbey, a piece of music, that the monks thought had been sent from heaven, began to be heard. They started to look for it and questioned the nephew of one of the canons who had previously been expelled. Caskets were found hidden in the dormitory ceiling. A miraculous force caused the locks to open and inside were the Saint's relics. A parchment was found, that proved the authenticity of the bones.

Religious feasts

The men of the Middle Ages liked religious feasts. The architecture of the Mont, with its huge church, mysterious crypts and great stairways, lent itself well to splendid ceremonies.

There were frequent processions through the abbey. The abbot then, just like a bishop, wore a mitre and carried a crook. The monks, instead of their severe, rough habits wore long, sleeveless cloaks known as albs. The whole monastery was lit up with candles. The relics in their reliquaries, and the Gospels, were taken among the pilgrims in the midst of clouds of incense. The procession came to a halt at special places where fervent prayers were said.

These ceremonies could turn into veritable theatrical shows. Monks played the parts of characters in the New Testament to help everyone understand the sacred texts, in the style of mystery plays held in front of cathedrals. In the 12th century, a monk from the Mont, who was a poet, wrote in the vernacular which all could understand (and not in Latin which was the language of the church), some verses which told the abbey's history and the miracles which had been wrought there. It was called the Roman du Mont Saint-Michel (The Story of the

Mont Saint-Michel) and was the work of a monk who had all the qualities of a real minstrel.

These ceremonies were always accompanied by singing, the monks' one passion. The human voice enhanced prayer. This plain song, or Gregorian chant, by virtue of its austerity and simplicity, was a form of worship in itself.

Finally, the reception of a new monk involved a moving ceremony. The young man's head was partly shaved : this was called the « tonsure », and was a symbol of his ecclesiastical calling. After one year's observation, he was allowed to take his vows in front of the whole community. The abbot helped him to put on a monk's habit to the accompaniment of songs of praise, and bestowed upon him a kiss of peace. For three days, he then prayed in the church. But after that, he was judged worthy to be a monk.

The abbey seen from the north-west, showing the Marvel and the church.

Mont Saint-Michel seen from the north-west, showing the gardens on the north side of the abbey.

The marvel

At the beginning of the 13th century, the great Anglo-Norman kingdom broke up. The King of France, Philippe-Auguste, took Normandy after a number of bloody battles. In the meantime, Mont Saint-Michel was besieged by an ally of the French King. The town and the abbey were in part destroyed by fire. In order to be pardoned and to convert the monastery to his cause, Philippe-Auguste sent a large amount of gold there, for it was necessary to rebuild.

A new art form, known later as « Gothic », was beginning to gain a hold. It was the age of the cathedral.

The « ogival » arch led to the construction of particularly spacious and high buildings. The abbots of the Mont and their architects concentrated on the monk's living quarters. This was how the « Merveille », or « Marvel », came to be built on the north side. It was a masterpiece of Gothic architecture. The Romanesque buildings were no longer large enough to accommodate the monks, whose numbers had increased, for they too were changing with the times and were concerned with more comfort and beauty to suit their life style.

The architects were certainly ambitious to dare to build such a high and vast building on this steep rock. Enormous buttresses were built on the outside to shore up the Marvel. But, at the same time, as the construction got higher, it had to become less and less massive, so as to forestall any possibility of collapse — a not infrequent occurence in the history of the Mont. The almonry and the store house on the bottom floor had very thick walls and strong vaults ; on the second floor, the Guests' room and the Knights' room had columns and ogival arches to support the third floor which contained the refectory and the cloister.

The stones arrived by sea at high tide from the Chausey Islands off the Mont. Stonemasons carved the granite into the correct shape. Sometimes they decorated it. Then with the help of ropes, pulleys or hoists such as the one that can still be seen at the Mont, the materials were hoisted up the scaffolding. When everything was assembled, the wooden supporting frames were removed.

The life of the monks

From now on, the monks spent most of their time in the Marvel. Poor pilgrims were welcomed in the almonry, rich ones on the floor above, in the Guests' room. Both places were near the entrance which, like it is today, was to the east, and not to the north-west as in the Romanesque era. The community kept well out of the way on the higher floors of the Marvel, near the church.

The thick walls of the refectory were pierced with long narrow windows that let in plenty of light, and supported a fine wooden « cradle » vault. Meals took place in silence while one monk read sacred texts from a pulpit situated on the south wall. The cloister, suspended in mid-air between sea and sky, was for talking a stroll, for meditation and conversation. The arcades are supported on fine columns of purple stone. Above the columns, the soft, white limestone of Caen has been

Mont Saint-Michel seen from the north.
Overleaf : *the marvel and the church.*

carved into flowers and leaves. These carvings are an admirable example of Norman decorative art.

Before the introduction of printing, the only way of preserving and reproducing a text was to copy it by hand. This was done by the monks, who went to great pains to decorate and beautify manuscripts. This was the art of illumination. Colours and designs were used to illuminate and illustrate individual letters. The Mont was known as the « city of books », for there were so many fine works in its library. The monks were not only interested in sacred texts and prayers, but also the works of Antiquity. The « chauffoir », or hot room, was the place where the monks conducted this meticulous work, as well as everything else. This room, that was later called the « Knights' », room, shows only too well that the monk's main enemy was the dank cold that came from the sea and the mist. They fought against it by lighting huge fires, and using tapestries and furs for insulation.

Pilgrimages

In the Middle Ages, it was considered a duty to go on a pilgrimage. The richest or the bravest went to the Holy Land, Rome or Compostella. Others had to be content with a sanctuary that was nearer home. The Mont Saint-Michel, of course, was a great Norman centre of pilgrimage, but it also attracted pilgrims from all over France and all of western Christendom. Christians went there to pray to the Archangel for their sins to be forgiven and for all their hopes to come true. Ill people especially hoped that a miracle would give them back their health, as used to happen in the legends emanating from the Mont.

Sometimes God's calling was sudden and inexplicable : a man could set off for the Mont in the middle of shoeing a horse, leaving the job unfinished. In 1333, the entire population of a village suddenly left for the

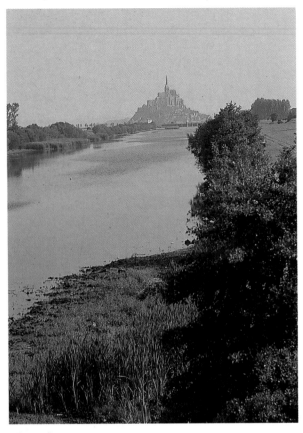

The R. Couesnon.

These roads were called « the ways of Paradise ».

He was threatened by many a danger, among them illness and fatigue. When he finally caught sight of the famous shape of the Mont he shouted out « Mont-joie », Mount Joy, in this great relief.

Miquelots at the mont

All kinds came to the Mont : invalids, pilgrims and wrong-doers mixed together, and all languages and dialects could be heard. Everyone was full of hope. Some wanted to repeat the experience of Norgod, Bishop of Avranches, who saw a bright light come down to the rock thereby revealing the presence of Saint Michael. Others even tried to spend the night in the dark church, only to give up after one of them was slapped by the invisible hand of God.

The pilgrim took part in the religious festivals. He tried to touch the reliquaries which contained the precious relics, the most curious of which were a tiny sword and shield that the archangel is said to have used to kill a dragon, and that had been brought by some miraculous means from a far-off country. The faithful pilgrim was also expected to make offerings : King Philip the Fair gave a statue covered in gold ; the poor made do with a piece of wax that went towards lighting the chapels.

The town nestling at the foot of the abbey welcomed the travellers. They dined in the taverns and slept in the hostelries. But important visitors were received by the abbot in the very large and bright Guests' room. Food was prepared in the two enormous hearths that were hidden from the rest of the room by sumptuous tapestries. Lavatories were installed in the north wall. The reception room with its elegant columns was richly adorned. Beneath it, however, near the entrance to the Gothic abbey, was the simple and austere almonry where the poorest people could get food.

Mont, forcing their parish priest to go with them and say Mass there.

A pilgrim on his way to the Mont was called a « miquelot ». Like all other pilgrims, he was recognisable by his leather sack that was carried over his right shoulder, and by his roughly hewn staff. He would also have shells, the very symbols of a pilgrimage, stitched to his clothing. A pilgrim could expect help and respect on his journey. He was given shelter for the night in special inns right the way along the roads leading to the Mont.

The abbey and the One Hundred Years' War

War broke out at the beginning of the 14th century between France and England, and took its toll together with the plague, which was then spreading throughout the whole of Christendom. It came to be called the « One Hundred Years' War ».

After the serious French defeats at Poitiers and Crécy, King Charles V began to make a comeback with the help of his constable, Bertrand Duguesclin. This

Breton knight was the captain of the Mont Saint-Michel. When he left France for Spain, he entrusted his wife, Tiphaine Raguenel, to the protection of Saint-Michael the Archangel. She lived in a house built at the top of the town, undertaking good works and practising the science of astrology which she was devoted to : she could read the future of the world in the movement of the stars.

On the occasion of one of his visits to the abbey, the mad King, Charles VI, made the abbot Pierre le Roi, who was an academic of some standing, into his counsellor. He immediately began to fortify the abbey. He defended the entrance by building towers, successive courtyards, and ramparts, thereby creating a veritable fort together with its « barbican ». He completed the living quarters on the south side. These were reserved for the abbot and for the administrative and judiciary offices.

Normandy fell into English hands in 1415, after the French defeat at Agincourt. The province was then governed by the Duke of Bedford, the brother of the English King, who succeeded in winning over to his cause a number of leading Norman personalities. Among them was the abbot of the Mont, Robert Jolivet, Pierre le Roi's successor, who accepted to be counsellor to Bedford, and received, in exchange, all the property belonging to the monastery.

The monks refused to support their treacherous abbot. Some knights, who had been dispossessed of their lands, had sought refuge with them, and they stayed faithful to the French cause, the only defender of which was the Dauphin Charles, who was later to become Charles VII, the so-called « King of Bourges ».

The Romanesque chancel at the Mont collapsed and, because of the war, it was impossible to reconstruct it. One of the Mont's captains died in combat ; the small island of Tombelaine fell into English hands ; and, as a sinister omen of things to come, the river Couesnon changed course after an unusually high tide.

The shepherd lads and lasses

During these troubled times in the first half of the XIVth century, a strange phenomenon occured. Despite all the dangers involved, children began to go on pilgrimage to the Mont Saint-Michel. They were called the « shepherd lads and lasses » in popular ballads and tales. A chronicle from the town of Cologne in Germany contains a description of these great child crusades : « That year, there was a great pilgrimage to the Mont Saint-Michel in Normandy, a pilgrimage that lasted about two years and which was made up of small children of eight, nine, ten and twelve years of age, that came from all the towns and villages of Germany and Belgium, and other countries too ». They gathered together in large numbers, abandonning their parents, and marched along, two by two, in procession. At the head of the column were students bearing effigies of Saint Michael. Children from the same area grouped together behind their own standard, which was decorated with the coats of arms of their local gentry. These children inspired pity, for they had left their homes against the wishes of their parents and without any money for the journey. Nevertheless, they remained in good health, for all along the road they were given food and drink in sufficient quantities. When they arrived at the Mont Saint-Michel, they offered their standards to the Archangel.

Mont Saint-Michel seen from the west.

The mass.

The siege of the mont

The beginning of the 15th century was a critical period for the Mont Saint-Michel.

The English decided to storm this stronghold which dared to stand up to them. A citadel that was defended both by its ramparts and by the sea was impregnable. It had to be surrounded and obliged to give itself up through famine and lack of water.

The siege began in 1424. Numerous troops took up positions around the Bay. A small wooden fort called the « bastille » was constructed at Ardevon, in front of the Mont, as a refuge in the event of an attack, and in order to keep a watch over the shore. Finally, a flotilla arrived to complete the blockade, from the sea.

Some Breton noblemen commanded an expedition from Saint-Malo and skilfully attacked the English ships and managed to disperse them. This naval victory enabled the Mont to receive provisions by sea. The siege had failed utterly and the citadel had not surrendered.

For the first time in a long while, the French were able to recover their confidence. It seemed that the Archangel himself had made this victory possible, and his cult won all the more prestige. This is why Saint Michael was among those who appeared to Joan of Arc. He told her : « I am Michael, the protector of France. Arise, and go to help the King of France ». And he guided the shepherd girl from Lorraine through her great adventures.

Charles VII put a very able captain, called Louis d'Estouteville, in charge of the Mont's garrison. He set about putting an end to the squabbles, schemings, pillaging and debauchery that were now common in the abbey, and had been introduced by rough, coarse soldiers who knew no better. Because he tightened up discipline in this way, the citadel was able to withstand the last attack by the English in 1433. A fire broke out in the town, destroying the wooden houses and damaging the ramparts. The English tried to take advantage of this by coming in large numbers with terrible war engines which succeeded in breaching the walls. For a while, they thought they had taken the town, but the garrison held on, and, in the end, the English were forced to withdraw. The shore was strewn with the dead, and the knights from the Mont retrieved two enormous cannons which were set up at the entrance to the town where they can still be seen.

The knights of Saint Michael

The King at the end of the Middle Ages, Louis XI, was an able but cruel monarch. He was very devout, and even superstitious. He loved pilgrimages, which is why he twice visited the sanctuary which symbolised the French victory over the English.

It was this that made him think of creating the Order of the Knights of Saint Michael, with the Archangel as its first member. The Duke of Burgundy, who was a great enemy of the King, already had the Knights of the Golden Fleece. But the Knights of Saint Michael were the King's own creation and were chosen from among the finest noblemen of the kingdom. They received a necklace of golden shells on which hung a medal which depicted Michael slaying the dragon, and had written on it the motto of the Order : « Immensi terror oceani » (the terror of the immense ocean).

The dignitaries wore white damask robes and a red velvet headdress. They took part in splendid ceremonies presided over by the King at the chapel of Saint Michael in the heart of Paris.

The King had another idea which was nothing short of lugubrious. He ordered a wood and metal cage to be suspended from the ceiling at the Mont. Every time the prisoner inside moved, the whole contraption began to rock. Being in this confined space in the freezing and lonely old abbey, was just like being in Hell. For centuries, political prisoners who had offended the King or his servants, were locked away there. Some were left for years at the mercy of the rats ; some ended up going mad.

The last constructions

Captain d'Estouteville had strengthened the abbey's defences. The town, which had always been threatened in war, had been encircled by ramparts and strong towers such as the Roy, Cholet, Beatrix and Arcade towers. With all its cannons, machicolations through which various objects could be dropped in defence, and watchtowers which commanded a view over the shores, the Mont Saint-Michel had become one of the strongest forts of its day. A lot of progress had been made during the long war in the art of attack and self-defence.

Abbot Jolivet had died at Rouen in the midst of the English whom he had served well. Louis d'Estouteville had appointed his brother, Guillaume, as abbot of the Mont. This man was a prince of the Church, a cardinal. He wasn't a monk but a priest. His many important commitments prevented him from devoting all his time to the monastery, which he left in the hands of the prior. Thus started the « commendam » system, which involved the abbot residing outside his community while receiving the greater part of their revenue. From that time on, the King handed over numerous abbeys to important people whom he wanted to honour or reward.

The everyday life of the monks.

The cardinal's prestige and his influence with the Pope and the King speeded up the reconstruction of the church. A crypt known as « the crypt of the wide pillars », supported the new construction which was finished at the beginning of the 16th century. The tall, graceful chancel is lit by high windows, and a gallery with delicate carvings and tracery. To support the building at the top of the rock, flying buttresses were positioned to act as props. The outside was finished off with « pinnacles », or fine pyramids decorated with flowers. Because of its rich profusion of detail, this style was known as the « flamboyant » style. A « lacework stairway » (the name is well chosen) gives access through this forest of granite right up to the roof, from where the whole sweep of the Bay can be seen.

The Wars of Religion

At the beginning of the 16th century, one of the king's lieutenants completed the defences of the town. From now on, the entrance to the town was well protected by the Avancée, Boulevard and Roy gates, which were reinforced by the addition of a moat, drawbridge and portcullis.

Throughout the century, the Kings of France visited the famous abbey, and François 1st was received there with great pomp. But the Wars of Religion threw the kingdom into confusion, and the Mont was caught up in a whirlwind of battles and massacres.

The Protestants tried to capture this Catholic stronghold. Since it was reputed to be impregnable, Captain Le Touchet endeavoured, in 1577, to take it through cunning. Men disguised as pilgrims hid their weapons and managed to get within the walls. They won over the soldiers watching the abbey gates by offering them wine, and then took up their positions on the Saut-Gauthier to await reinforcements. A novice (future monk) from the abbey realised what they were up to and gave the alarm. The monk alerted the townspeople at the foot of the monastery. When they realised they had been discovered, the false pilgrims tried to bluff their way out by shouting « the town has been taken », but the inhabitants took up their arms to help the monks. Captain Le Touchet, who was just arriving with his horsemen, had to turn back, leaving his companions to surrender.

Another stratagem was used later by members of the formidable Montgomery family. Men disguised as women and fishermen approached the Mont. The guards at the town gate grew suspicious and killed them all in cold blood. The Huguenot troops appeared from nowhere and took the town. But the abbey continued to resist. The military governor was away from the Mont at the time, but as soon as he received news of what was happening, he gathered some men and rushed back. They hoisted themselves up, with the help of ropes, to the ramparts above the occupied town and started a counter-offensive. The Protestants, caught between two lines of fire, were defeated, and all the prisoners were locked up on Tombelaine Island.

A copy of the model of Mont Saint-Michel.

The abbey in ruins

Monastic life was on the wane. The monks began to abandon their abbey : some of them preferred to live in the taverns. They were no longer respected. The abbots, such as Abbot de Guise or Cardinal de Montmorency, were selected by the King from amongst the finest nobility. But they no longer visited the Mont : they were quite content to collect some of its revenue. An unexpected revival took place when new Benedictines, the Maurists, took it over. These learned men were devoted to the history of the Mont, which they studied from the collection of manuscripts that had been built up over the ages.

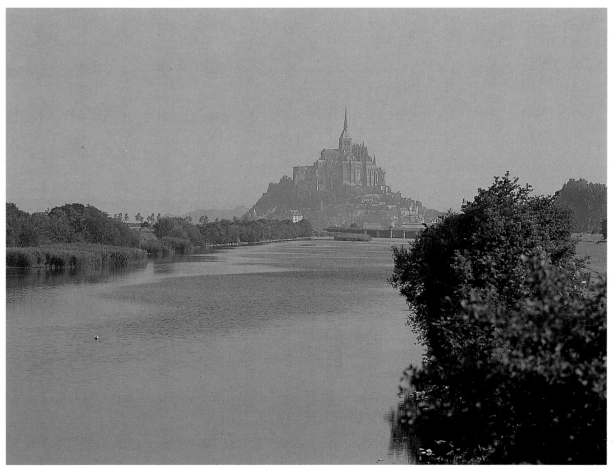

Mont Saint-Michel seen from the mainland.

Overleaf : *Mont Saint-Michel seen from the north-west.*
In the foreground are St. Aubert's Chapel
and the Gabriel Tower.

The buildings were badly maintained and virtually falling into ruin. Both the high towers and three supporting arches in the church collapsed. They were not rebuilt in their original style but replaced in 1780 by a very simple Classical façade.

Meanwhile, the abbey was transformed into a prison and became the « sea Bastille ». Writs were issued by the King to banish to the island without fair trial, debauched aristocrats, corrupt priests and political opponents. The worst of them were shut up in dank, dark dungeons, or, indeed, in Louis XI's famous cage.

The resurrection of the Mont

The French Revolution got rid of the last of the monks but the Mont Saint-Michel continued to be a prison. From now on, the whole abbey was a new batch of political prisoners. Victor Hugo evoked the tragic fate of those men : « All around us, as far as the eye can see, infinite space, the blue horizon of the sea, the green horizon of the land, clouds, air, liberty, birds wheeling, ships at full sail ; and then suddenly,

The island of Tombelaine.

over the top of the old wall above our heads, the pale face of a prisoner ».

The abbey was rediscovered by visitors and Romantic writers during the 19th century. They admired the extraordinary architecture. This was the birth of tourism. The prison was abolished under the Second Empire. In 1874, the Mont had become a « historic monument ».

The Mont Saint-Michel rose again from its ruins. Restoration was undertaken, with extreme attention to detail. The Gothic steeple was rebuilt, thus giving the finishing touch to the famous silhouette rising above the sand. A single monk, and then a little community, came and revived the religious tradition. This abbey, which is also a citadel, bears witness to one thousand years of effort to please God, monks and pilgrims alike.

The island of Tombelaine

Tombelaine means « small tomb ». Like the Mont, its is an outcrop of granite spared from erosion by the sea. Today, it is deserted. Yet for many years, it was a modest reflection of the great abbey that was its neighbour. A chapel and a priory were built on it and used by the monks for retreats. A Venitian philosopher worked there. Gradually, this island too became a fortress. The English captured it during the One Hundred Years' War and from there threatened the Mont's garrison. In the 17th century, the fortress belonged to Fouquet and, when the Superintendant of Finances fell into disgrace, Louis XIV had the fortifications razed to the ground. Thereafter, Tombelaine where, according to legend, King Arthur's fiancee, Hélène, died, disappeared from the pages of the history books.

A GUIDED TOUR OF MONT SAINT-MICHEL

Let us now look at the main features on any tour of the Mont. After passing through the town gates, the street rises up to the abbey. Our tour follows the traditional route but is only intended as a suggestion. Once you have seen the monastery, you should leave yourself time to stroll through the town and along the top of the town walls.

The town gates

One of the major preoccupations of men in the Middle Ages was how to fortify the entrance to their town. Three huge gates were built to provide increased resistance to attack - the Forward, Boulevard and King's Gates. The third line of defence was the King's Gate (Porte du Roy) protected on the south side by the two great Arcade and King's Towers. A moat, drawbridge and portcullis made it even more difficult for attackers to enter the town. The coats-of-arms of the abbey, the town and the monarch, the symbols of the three levels of authority, were all carved on the gateway. The guards kept watch from the top of the parapet walk and were billetted in the King's Lodging. Leading up to this gate was the Boulevard and its gate, which were also designed in the 15th century. One hundred years later, the king's lieutenant completed the defensive system by building the Forward Gate (Porte de l'Avancée). The « bourgeoisie », i.e. the local population, were required to take turns to keep watch from this gate, which is flanked by the Bourgeois' Guardroom. In 1434, fire raged through the town. The locals, who had already withstood a siege lasting several years, seemed to lost all hope. The English launched an attack on the fortress, using an awesome display of weaponry, but they were repulsed. The victors carried off cannon known as michelettes or miquelettes. War had created its own means of destruction and the intense fire power of these bombards made it essential to strengthen the town walls and the entire system of defence.

The Forward Gate.

The Boulevard Gate.

The English bombards.

The King's Gate.

The abbey seen from the north-east, showing the entrance, the forework, the Corbins' Tower and the Marvel.

The entrance to the abbey

There is no doubt about it - the Abbey is a citadel. Although the steep sides of the rock made attack difficult, men throughout the ages have tried their best to give the monastery added protection. The Romanesque buildings already had a good system of defence. The Gothic « Marvel » with its three storeys, proud walls and mighty buttresses, gives every appearance of being impregnable.

With the first rumours of war came the continuation of military effort and, in the late 14th century, Pierre le Roi had the redoubt built. In front of it is a rectangular forework with crenelated walls, the barbican. It is flanked by two fine turrets, built to either side of the entrance itself. The staircase that leads up to the Guardroom was once closed off by a portcullis. The steps are particularly steep and have been compared to an « abyss ». Near the south postern gate (a fortified entrance) on the redoubt is an old tavern called « The Spinning Sow » (La Truie qui file).

After the long siege of the Mont by the English, Captain Louis d'Estouteville designed a first-class system of defence. All the ramparts were strengthened between 1425 and 1440, and the entire town was surrounded by a wall. As firearms had become more reliable thanks to improvements made during various conflicts, the design allowed for their use here - they were, after all, an active means of defence. Gunports abound on the

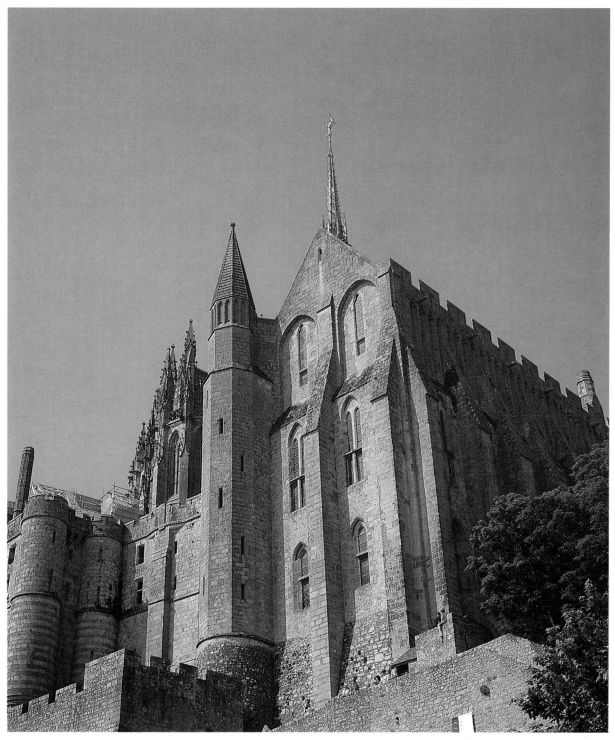

Mont, and the cannon were ready to repulse any attack.

The original entrance to the abbey lay to the northeast before being moved to the east. The gatehouse is on the ground floor, and it contains the finest fireplace in the monastery, decorated with luxurious moulding. From 1364 onwards, visitors were required to leave their weapons here and, at the end of the 14th century, when the Mont became a citadel, the gatehouse was turned into the Guardroom. With its tall, storeyed vaulting,

Above : *the ramparts seen from the Great Outer Staircase.*

Opposite : *the Great Inner Staircase seen from Gautier's Leap (to the left is the almonry water tank dating from the 16th century).*

Right : *the Great Inner Staircase and the abbey lodgings.*

it opens onto the main inner staircase, the abbot's lodging and the Gothic almonry.

The Great Outer Staircase leads from the town to the Abbey.

In the Middle Ages, « entry » into a town or abbey involved grandiose ceremonial if the visitor was powerful and famous. It was a sacred act and was eventually subject to rules laid down by tradition. The king was received at the town gates, the Archbishop of Rouen at the top of the town, and the Bishop of Avranches at the entrance to the abbey itself. The entrance ceremony was a reflection of social hierarchy and, because of this, the architecture had to provide a majestic backdrop to the slow climb up the rock. The Great Inner Staircase, with its landings and wide steps, was an integral part of the ceremony.

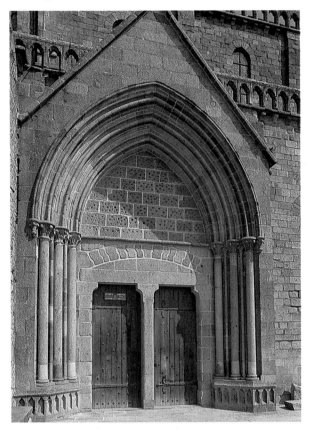

It runs alongside the abbey lodgings, forming the « worldly » part of the abbey which is in permanent contact with visitors.

The staircase also had a defensive role. To reach the church, attackers would have to pass through here, along what was, in fact, a ditch between two high walls. Monks or soldiers could defend it from the two fortified bridges connecting the lodgings to the interior of the church. The stone bridge with machicolations was built in the 15th century and its military function is quite obvious. The other bridge was built of timber and slate, in the 16th century. The Main Staircase leads to the terrace known as « Gautier's Leap » (Saut-Gautier) and the southern door to the church.

The abbey church

Building began on the church in the 11th century but the original construction was fragile and required alteration on several occasions over the years.

Opposite : *the South Door in the church.*

Below : *The West Front.*

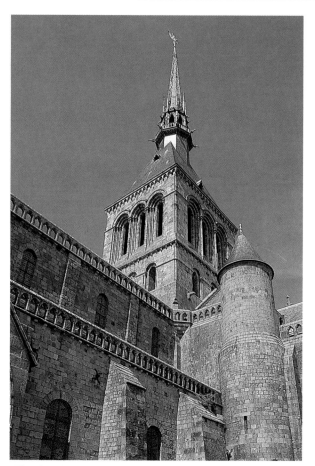

The church tower.

The belltower

Lightning struck the church tower on numerous occasions, setting fire to the fragile wooden construction. In the Gothic period, a tall spire was built, flanked by six small pyramidal towers. In the 17th century, an onion dome was erected and a platform was built onto it in the 18th century for the Chappe telegraph. Finally, the architect Petitgrand designed the present tower. Above its two « Romanesque » storeys is a Gothic spire which is a copy of the one on Notre-Dame cathedral in Paris. It is topped by a statue of St. Michael brandishing his lance as he slays the dragon - a piece of sculpture by Frémiet. And so Mont Saint-Michel acquired its final outline.

The arms of the abbey

This coat-of-arms surrounded by carved drapes was placed at the entrance to the church in the 18th century, behind the new West Front. The abbey's arms took many years to achieve their final form. In the 15th century, they consisted of three shells. They then became a « sprinkling of sable (i.e. black) shells bearing at their head (in a horizontal band) the fleur-de-lys of France ». The abbey became a centre of pilgrimage very early on in its existence, as is shown by the shells which were the distinguishing mark of pilgrims all along their route. The fleurs-de-lys, the symbol of the French monarchy, were then added to the arms. They proclaimed the King of France as the pro-

The abbey's coat-of-arms.

The West Front and the original layout

From the 16th to 19th centuries, the buildings fell into disrepair. The first three spans of the church were demolished in the 18th century. The Classical facade was completed in 1780. Its austerity and unobtrusiveness is particularly well-suited to the Mont. The Romanesque facade was also very plain. It was flanked by two towers that were reminiscent of the ones in Jumièges ; they were built during the abbacy of Robert de Thorigny. One of them was demolished in the Middle Ages ; the other one, the Clock Tower on the south side, survived until the fire in 1776. The first spans of the church were replaced by this west-facing platform called the « Plomb du Four », the « end of the nave ». The platform looks westward towards the Isles Chausey which provided the granite for the buildings on the Mont. The present sacristy on the left of the West Front was originally the monks' dorter. It forms the upper storey of the Romanesque monastery buildings. The short distance separating it from the church enabled the monks to go to the sanctuary in the dark to hear Matins.

tector of the monastery and fortress. The crozier and mitre, which were sometimes added for decoration, showed the rank of the abbot who was « mitred and croziered » i.e. of equivalent rank to a bishop. Each abbot also had his own family coat-of-arms which he often included in the stained glass windows in the church.

The Romanesque nave (11th century)

Mediaeval architects brought a sense of movement into the church by breaking up the impression of length with arches and the appearance of height with upper storeys.

The nave originally had seven arches or spans, and was

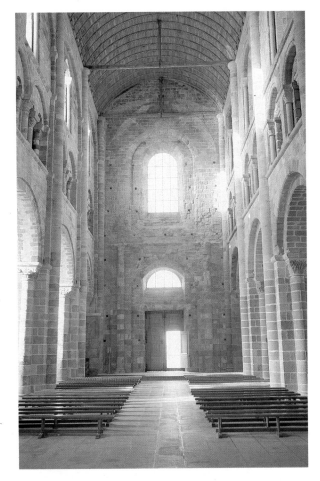

The Romanesque nave in the minster.

Right : *the north side*
of the Romanesque nave (12th century).

completed c. 1084. At that time, Norman architecture was in its heyday, thanks to the Abbot-Architect, William of Volpiano. The Normans only used vaulting in the « most sacred » parts of their church. In the nave, they were

content with timber rafters, which had the advantage of forming a lighter barrel vault on the narrow surface of the rock.

The ceiling in the church may originally have been flat. The timber vaulting is thought to have been built in the 15th century.

The transept crossing was built in 1138 on the orders of Bernard du Bec. It has ogival vaulting, a precursor of things to come. When carving out the space for the bell in the late 19th century, the architect-in-charge, Petit-grand, totally restored this section with its four pillars.

The Romanesque chancel also had a vaulted roof but it collapsed in the 15th century. Was it a Benedictine chancel with two spans and two side aisles leading into the apse ? Or, as a miniature in the Heures du Duc de Berry would seem to suggest, did the chancel have an ambulatory ?

The north wall of the Romanesque nave (12th century)

The nave in Mont Saint-Michel minster shows the progress made in architecture during the Romanesque period. Thereafter, the solidity of the building was based on a framework of pillars and arches rather than on a huge pile of stone. Weight and thrust were taken into consideration. « The entire building then becomes an active organism, not a passive force. A piece of masonry becomes a piece of architecture » (German Bazin).

This slenderness, elegance and regularity were not achieved without disasters. One morning in 1103, while the monks were at prayer, the north wall of the nave collapsed onto the monastery buildings. It had to be rebuilt, thicker and with fewer openings. The south section of the nave, then, dates from the 11th century while the north wall is 12th century.

In each span, three storeys are marked out by horizontal banding - the great arches, the triforium above, and the clerestorey at the top which lets in the light. Each span is topped by a large relieving arch. By bearing all the weight of the rafters, this arch enabled the builder to raise only a thin wall between the pillars. The other unusual feature is the long engaged pillar which rises to the very top of the church, forming a veritable « inner buttress ».

The pillars in the chancel (mid 15th century)

When the pillars in the chancel reached gallery level, the work was stopped and it did not begin again until the early 16th century. These ten pillars gave the chancel a

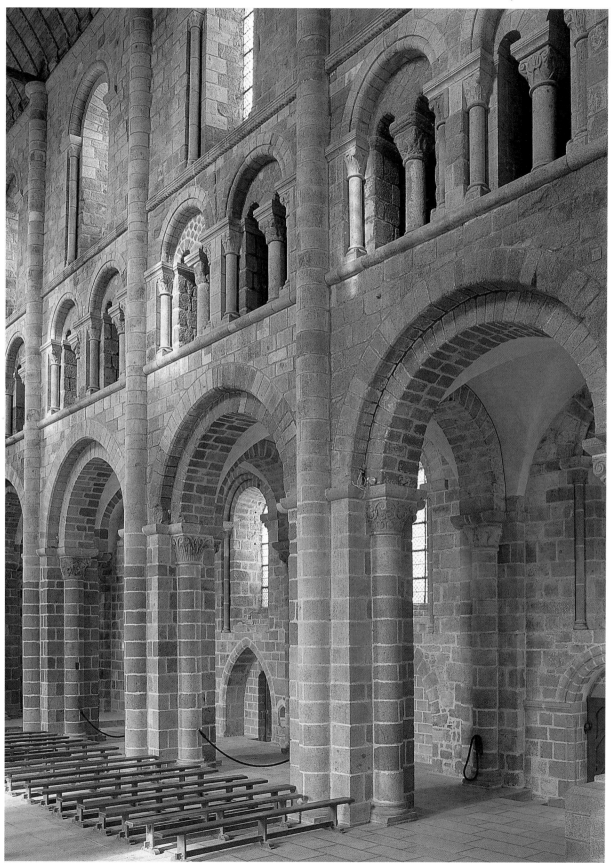

polygonal layout. Each pillar is shaped like a diamond and consists of a sheaf of colonettes, all of them similar in appearance. Each colonette corresponds to one base of the ogival vaulting or arches. All these details create a sense of organic logic in this perfect example of architecture at its best. An ambulatory runs round the chancel, with radiating chapels. At the end of the church, in the chapel behind the High Altar, is a piscina, decorated with floral motifs. It was designed to hold holy water. The chapel was known in the 17th century as Notre-Dame-du-Circuit, the « circuit » being the ambulatory.

The Flamboyant Gothic Chancel (1450-1521)

Its design was based on the nave in St. Ouen's Abbey in Rouen where Guillaume d'Estouteville was also Abbot. The original plans may have been drawn up by the same architect, Guillaume Pontis. St. Ouen's was considered in the late Middle Ages as one of the finest examples of Gothic architecture then in existence. The 15th-century project for the Mont was scrupulously adhered to, although the building work was completed by Guillaume and Jean de Lamps in the early 16th century. Four centuries, then, separate the Romanesque nave and

The triforium.

The Flamboyant Gothic chancel.

Right : the lace stairway and the pinnacles on the chevet.

the chancel that may be seen as a final expression of mediaeval architecture.

Everything has been sacrificed to the sense of verticality. The pillars are devoid of capitals. The narrowness of the arches in comparison to their height emphasises the impression of an upward vertical swing. Each span is also broken up by three storeys i.e. the arches, the triforium or blind storey, and the clerestorey.

The triforium

The triforium, which is supported by the pillars in the ambulatory, skirts the pillars to avoid weakening them. The openwork in the gallery lets light flood in. Flamboyant Gothic architecture turned this into a fine piece of stone tracery with a balustrade over three-lobed arches and numerous lancets (elongated ogival arches) topped by a frieze. The ogival arches top the « glass cage » as F. Enaud termed the top of the chancel. They are interconnected by keystones bearing the coats-of-arms of the abbey, Jean Le Veneur, and St. Michael slaying the dragon.

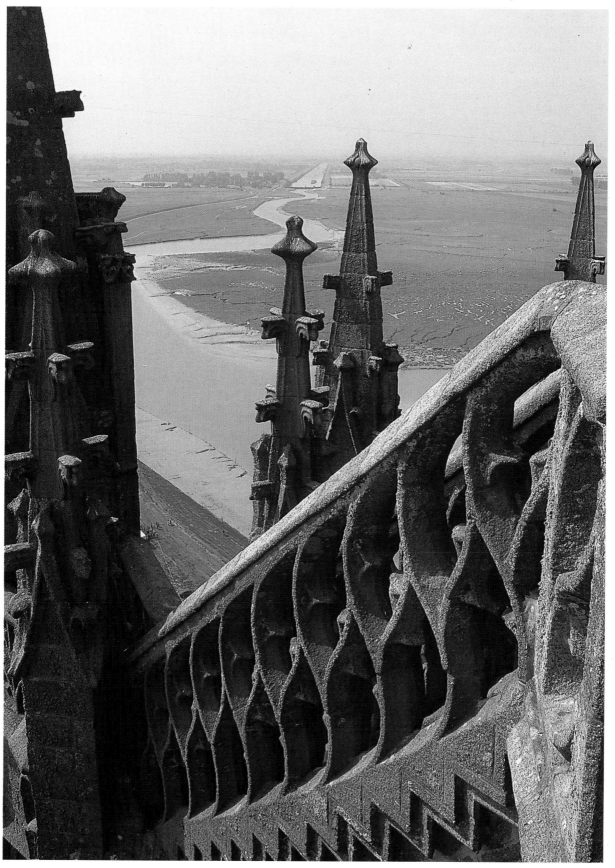

The lace staircase

A staircase was built in one pier on the chevet that was thicker than the others. It leads to a walkway high above the ground, connected to the roof of the chancel. The Flamboyant Gothic style demanded that the granite of the handrail and the finialed pinnacles be traceried. Through this piece of lacework carved in stone, there is a superb view right across Mont Saint-Michel Bay with its sandbanks and pools of water.

The chevet (early 16th century)

The unusually high vaulting in the chancel had a tendency to lean outwards and it had, therefore, to be counterbalanced. Flying buttresses were used as stone props. Oblique forces are transmitted to enormous vertical buttresses, made up of two piers that are veritable aerial pillars, joined by a wall with tracery at the top and coping above it. The piers rest on the dividing walls in the radiating chapels and are therefore laid out in a fan shape. If the chevet as we see it is a « forest of stone », it is because prudence had become the architect's watchword for fear of further catastrophe.

The piers around the chevet are topped by pinnacles, pyramids ornamented with stone flowers that bear witness to the decorative genius of the period.

The Romanesque abbey buildings and crypts

In the Romanesque period (11th century), the abbey entrance lay on the north-west side of the rock. The buildings consisted of three storeys, with the dorter beside the church situated above the monks' gallery that was itself built on top of the Aquilon Chamber.

The abbot, Robert de Thorigny, had his lodgings built on the west side.

The minster is supported by crypts such as Our Lady of the Thirty Candles (Notre-Dame des Trente Cierges) which lies beneath the north arm of the transept. This chapel, where the Virgin Mary's clothes were once kept, was the spiritual heart of the abbey. The vestibule has a central pillar decorated with Gothic foliage and was once used as a prison. In those days, it was known as the « Devil's Dungeon ».

The monks' gallery (12th century)

This long chamber beneath the dorter represents a turning-point in architectural design. Roger II originally had groined arches built but Bernard du Bec had them replaced by ogival arching after a fire in 1138. Two arches set between transverse ribs cross each other diagonally. This technique, which gives the vaulting greater fullness, is a forerunner of Gothic architecture. The two aisles separated by five pillars stand above the rock to the east and the Aquilon Chamber to the west.

The capitals are decorated with plant motifs in the form of stylised leaves and fleurs-de-lys. The decoration is sometimes straight, and sometimes set upside down. The corners of some of the capitals also have carvings of human beings putting their arms beneath their legs ; others have motifs in the shape of purses. Two bay windows let light into the chamber.

Nobody knows what the chamber was originally intended to be used for. Tradition has it that this was the Romanesque cloister where the monks relaxed and took a stroll, hence its name. The adjoining buildings, which have been mutilated, are said to have been the refectory and kitchen. The Maurists turned them into latrines.

The Aquilon chamber (12th century) [photo page 38]

The name of an icy blast was given to the Romanesque almonry because it lay on the north side of the rock. Since the original entrance to the abbey was on

The chevet.

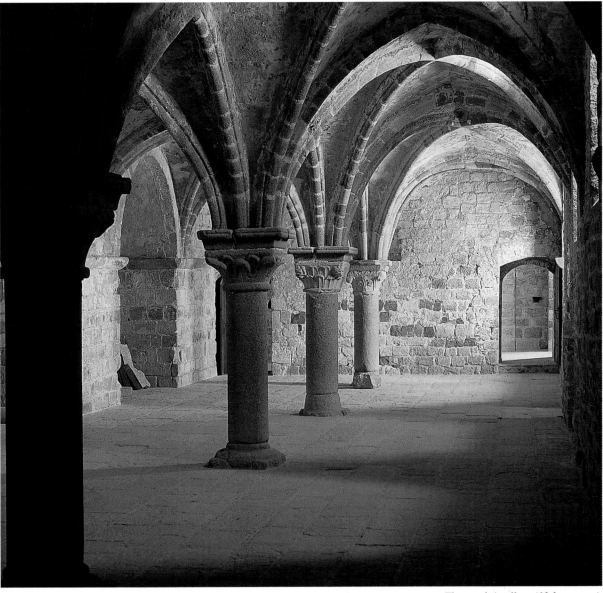

The monks' gallery (12th century).

the north-west side, it was in this room that pilgrims were welcomed to the Mont. It was not connected to the monastery buildings in order to prevent any disruption to the solitude of the brothers. This means that the staircase leading to the monks' gallery is a more recent addition.

After the fire of 1112, Abbot Roger II had the wooden roof replaced by stone vaulting, in an effort to decrease the fire hazard. The vaulting is groined and is formed by the penetration of two barrel vaults within the same semicircle. The austere capitals are decorated with swirls and a central heart-shaped motif.

Robert de Thorigny's apartments (late 12th century)

Pilgrims arriving at the Mont followed long vaulted galleries to the south side of the abbey. The Romanesque abbot's lodgings stood at the south-west and were three storeys high. This was the seat of temporal life in the monastery. The Abbot lived here, welcomed visitors here, passed judgement here, and meted out punishment here. On the upper floor, beneath the platform at the West Front of the minster, were two rooms designed for the Abbot's Court. When the Mont was used as a prison, the famous « iron cage » used to be hung from

The Aquilon Chamber (or Romanesque almonry).

places. The Cyclopean wall at the end of the chapel may be a throwback to the former oratory dating from the 8th and 9th centuries. The church, which originally stood in the open air, became a crypt when the Romanesque nave was built above it. It was badly damaged in the 18th century then restored in the 20th. Prestressed concrete was used to bear the weight of the minster above.

The wheel, the hoist (19th century) and the Romanesque ossuary

The Romanesque abbey was extended on the south side by buildings designed to accommodate pilgrims but the three storeys collapsed in 1817. The only reminder of them these days is a model kept in the Invalides Museum. The infirmary opened onto St. Stephen's Chapel, the mortuary chapel where, it is thought, cadavers may have been laid out. It had 13th-century ogival vaulting. The monks' ossuary was next to the chapel. Death, then, was an integral part of the architecture. The prison service installed a huge wheel in this ossuary and prisoners walked inside it to make it turn. A trolley would then be drawn up along a hoist, a veritable stone ladder snaking its way up the wall of rock. It

The great tread wheel.

the 11th-century barrel vaulting. Robert de Thorigny commissioned the building of his austere apartments further west, in the 12th century. They looked out to sea and it was here that he received a visit from the King, Henri II, in 1158. On the lower storey near the door was the gatehouse. The porter could keep a watchful eye on travellers passing beneath the porch beyond the canopy near the Aquilon Chamber. Two dungeons, nicknamed « Vade in pace », were built into the ground here when the abbey was turned into the « Bastille of the Sea ». They were known familiarly as the « twins ».

Our Lady Underground (mid 10th century)

Notre-Dame-sous-la-Terre is the Preromanesque church. It was built in the middle of the 10th century, at the same time as the abbey was founded. Its two parallel aisles are separated by a wall consisting of two arches. Carolingian traditions are apparent in several

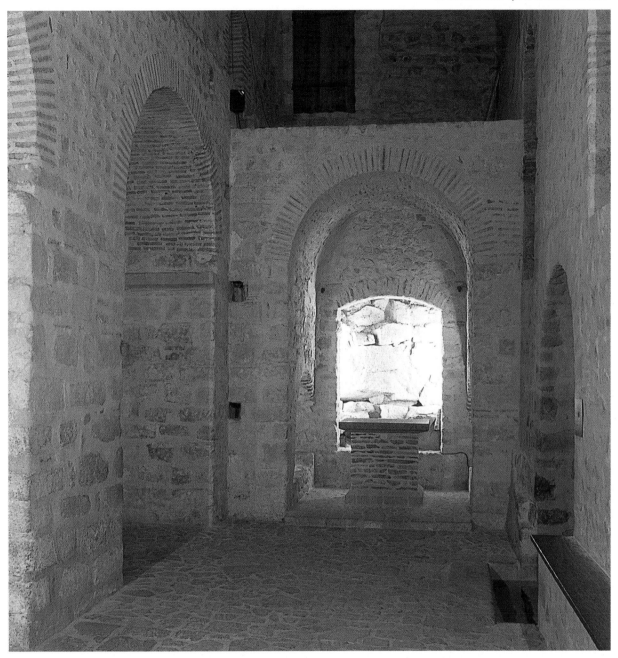

The Chapel of Our Lady Underground.

Overleaf : *the Gothic cloisters.*

was, in fact, a reminder of the Middle Ages since it re-sembled the wheel used by the monks. One of them was in use for many years in the Romanesque undercroft and there was a second one in the Gothic undercroft in the Marvel. It was this latter system which was used by a captain during the Wars of Religion in his attempt to enter the citadel.

St Martin's chapel

The St. Martin crypt bears the weight of the south transept of the abbey church. Its semicircular barrel vaulting is a model of rigourous austerity. The Christian liturgy preferred crypts, which were places of medita-tion and prayer.

The stone vaulting was the most important feature

of the mediaeval architecture. The dim atmosphere was particularly well-suited to the funeral rites to which the abbey devoted itself. The noblemen of the day preferred to be laid to rest in the shade of a church. The vaulting also improved the acoustics. And, after all, plainsong was the monks' only passion.

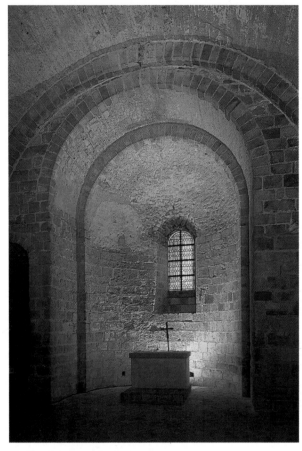

St. Martin's Chapel.

Right : *the Crypt of the Mighty Pillars.*

Indeed, it may arguably have been their supreme contribution to the arts.

The Crypt of the Mighty Pillars (1446-1450)

The Romanesque chancel collapsed in 1421 but war made rebuilding impossible. Once peace had been restored, Cardinal d'Estouteville, the influential abbot of the Mont, ordered the work to begin. The Crypt of the Mighty Pillars (*Crypte des Gros Piliers*) was erected in only a few years and was designed to support the new chancel. Ten enormous cylindrical columns were built, perhaps around the original Romanesque pillars. Two of them, which are smaller than the others, were given the descriptive name « palm trees ». Prism-sha-

ped ribs bring life to the vaulting, penetrating the pillars or walls at their base. Flamboyant Gothic architecture imposed its skilful techniques and its sense of aesthetics with the art of carving voussoirs (stones in vaulted roofs carved in the shape of a corner) and the precise adjustment of the stonework allied to a preference for sharp, rather than rounded, forms.

The Marvel

The « Marvel » is the Gothic part of the abbey. It was built after the abbey was destroyed in the early years of the 13th century, replacing the Romanesque monastery buildings which had become too small and were totally lacking in amenities. The view here shows the east wing, the first to be built. Above a wide bank, there are three storeys symbolising the social hierarchy of the Middle Ages. The poor were given food on the lowest storey, in the almonry where the groined vaulting was reminiscent of traditional Romanesque architecture. On the second storey, the abbot welcomed rich, influential visitors, in the Guests' Chamber, where the vaulting is ogival. Finally, the refectory was the monks' dining hall - and the clergy were considered to take priority over all other members of society in mediaeval times. Wooden rafters were selected for this chamber in order to avoid weakening the building as a whole. The building was supported by massive external piers.

The western section of the Marvel was built after the east wing and had three storeys. At the top were the cloisters, beneath them was the Knights' Chamber with its huge bay window, and below that was the undercroft which was used as a cellar. Supplies were heaved up from the sand below by means of a great wheel. A drawbridge had been slung between two massive buttresses that supported the building on the north side. This wing of the abbey was reserved for the brothers, and formed the backcloth to their monastic life. It was intended to build a third group of buildings even further west, to include the chapter house where the community would hold its meetings and assemblies but the project was abandoned. At the most inaccessible spot, in the north-west corner, was the charter-room where the monastery archives were kept, proof of its wealth and its past heritage. This small airy room stands on top of an enormous corner pier.

The cloisters (early 13th century) [photo pages 40-41]

This was the place for exercise, conversation and meditation. It forms the top floor of the Marvel and it was reserved for the monks. The garth, which seems to hang in midair between the sea below and the sky above, is surrounded by covered walkways. It lies on the same level as the refectory and the church and rests on the vaulting in the Knights' Chamber. In or-

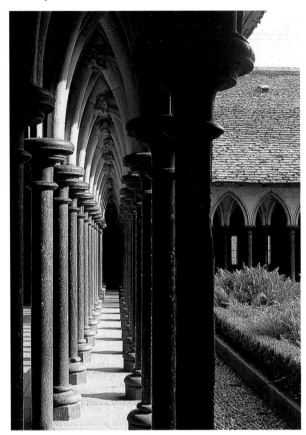

The colonettes in the cloisters.

A squinch in the cloisters.

der to lay out this area, which was both open and enclosed, the north transept of the abbey church was shortened at the spot where a huge Gothic window was built. The lavatorium, or lavabo, was built here with a double bench and a fountain, all at ground level. The abbot would celebrate the ceremony of the Washing of the Feet here, in memory of Christ. The monks also washed here before meals. Originally, the western gallery was intended to open onto the chapter house but it was never built. What would have been the doorways to the chapter house are now three bay windows.

The colonettes in the cloisters

The shafts may have been carved in England and imported into France. Originally, they were probably made of a fine-grained limestone similar to marble. But the architect, Corroyer, preferred a fine-grained granite. The hardness of this stone explains the prismatic outline and the simplicity of the plinths, bases and abaci. The colonettes were placed in staggered lines i.e. instead of being in pairs, they are in two rows that are slightly out of line with each other. They are connected by arches along the same two rows, and

«diagonal» arches mark out small triangular vaults. This succession of tripods gives the building absolute stability, since the weight and load are regularly distributed. The technique, which was quite unknown in cloisters before this date, was nevertheless fairly commonplace in Norman Gothic architecture where it was frequently incorporated into doorways. As this style of architecture did not lend itself to empty spaces, large crochets decorated with foliage were carved beneath the arches.

A squinch in the cloisters

Between the arches in the cloisters, the soft Caen limestone squinches have been ornamented with carvings, fairly conclusive proof, if any was needed, of the extent to which Norman architecture was fond of stone tracery. Two designs were chosen i.e. a rose surrounded by three other smaller roses, and a leaf pattern that fills the entire triangular section. The plant theme predominated, especially the vine, because it gave great scope for the sculptor's imagination. The cavity carved out in the wall provides a dark background from which the swirls of the carvings stand out. A frieze runs along the cloister walls above the squinches.

The cloisters are on the upper storey on the west side of the Marvel.

The Knight's Chamber is on the intermediate level of the Marvel, on the west side.

The refectory (early 13th century)

Monastic meals were veritable ceremonials. It took major feats of technical skill to embellish the room in which they were taken. Setting aside any question of a vaulted ceiling which would probably have been too heavy, the architects preferred to erect semi-circular rafters, a huge upturned hull built in the Gothic period but that was nevertheless reminiscent of the nave in the Romanesque part of the church. A thick wall bore this continual weight and, in order to avoid weakening it with huge bays, narrow windows scarcely wider than slits were built. Set deep in the walls, they are invisible from the entrance to the refectory although they provide an astonishing amount of light. Each of them is flanked by slender colonettes. Meals were taken in silence while one of the monks aloud read from holy texts. The pulpit stands in the south wall and, thanks to the excellent acoustics, the entire chamber was filled with his voice. The cellarer's office and kitchen were on the south side of the refectory.

The Knights' Chamber (early 13th century)

The chamber (*Salle des Chevaliers*) owes its name to the order of chivalry instituted by Louis XI, the Knights of St. Michael. Yet it seems that no meeting was ever held here. This was, in fact, the « calefactory ». Huge fireplaces, with a mantelpiece rising to the roof, afforded some protection against the cold. Tapestries divided the chamber off into small

The undercroft is on the lower storey of the Marvel.

The monks' refectory .

The monks' refectory is on the upper storey on the east side of the Marvel.

The Guests' Chamber is on the intermediate storey on the east side of the Marvel.

The Gothic almonry is on the lower storey.

rooms. They also hid the raised passageway to the south, along which guests went on their way to the church without disturbing the monks. The chamber was also the « main work room », the scriptorium, a quite different place to the ordinary calefactory in Benedictine monasteries. It was here that the monks copied and illuminated manuscripts.

The originality of Norman architecture comes to the fore here. It is sturdiness, rather than elegance, which prevails, and the development in design ideas is quite obvious when this chamber is compared to the Guests' Chamber built in an earlier period. Here, the pillars are stocky and the outline of the ogival vaulting is more noticeable. The torus, the major piece of moulding, is set off by two deep grooves. Lastly, the almost vertical capitals are decorated with fine carvings of foliage.

Right :
the abbey lodgings.

A fireplace in the Knights' Chamber.

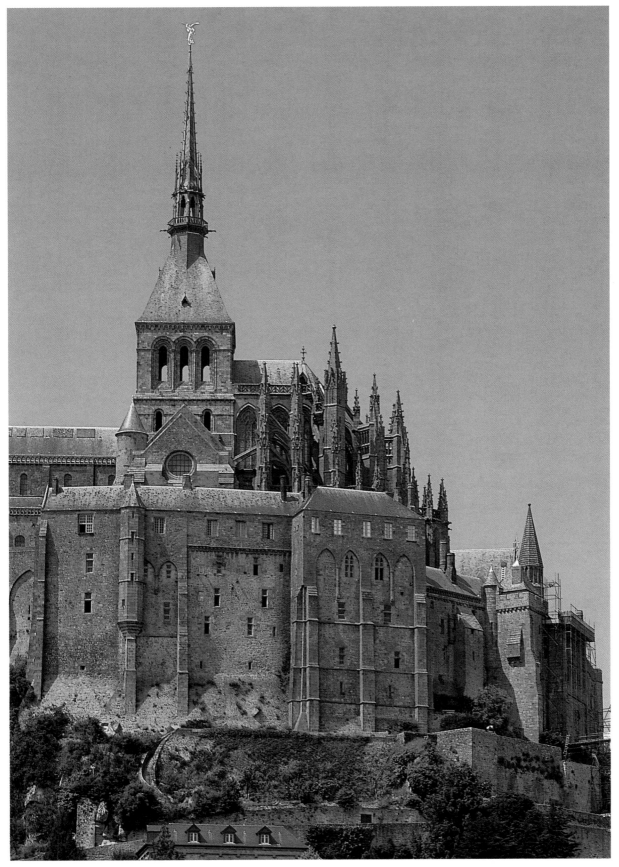

The Guests' Chamber (early 13th century)

Built by Abbot Raoul des Isles, this chamber (*Salle des Hôtes*) was intended for rich or famous visitors who took their meals here with the abbot. Two aisles in which the tables were set out, two huge fireplaces where the meals were prepared and which were separated from the rest of the chamber by tapestries, and latrines in the north wall - these were the necessary « mod. cons. » in any reception room of the day. The elegance of the ogival arches and pillars, the light flooding in through the great east-facing bay windows, the beauty of the stylised foliage, and the other decorative features that have since disappeared (paintings, tiling, stained glass, and tapestries) all made Gothic architecture a means of displaying enormous wealth. Using a style that originated in the Paris Basin, this chamber was « one of the most elegant creations of vernacular architecture in the Middle Ages » (Germain Bazin.) and was a forerunner of Royaumont and Ourscamp. The Guests' Chamber is preceded on the south side by the Chapel of St. Madeleine where travellers prayed both before and after meals.

The abbot's lodging

The abbot lived in close proximity to the pilgrims, while the monks sought peace in the « enclosure » on the north side. The various parts of the abbey can be

« read » from right to left, i.e. from East to South. Beyond the Marvel and the forework are the abbey lodgings, the « worldly » part of the abbey, built in stages between the 13th and 16th centuries. The Courtroom lies above the Guardroom. Known as Belle-Chaise, it has narrow windows separated by colonettes. The garrison was billetted in the Perrine Tower, a massive square construction with a pointed roof built by Pierre le Roi. This tower is immediately adjacent to the residence occupied by the Bailiff, a lay officer within the community. Beyond it were the Abbot's apartments, in an impressive residence supported by three piers and four relieving arches. During the days of the monarchy, political prisoners were detained here, in Minor and Major Exile. Finally, there is the Chapel of St. Catherine of the Steps (*Sainte-Catherine-des-Degrés*) and the last building, the Priory, near Gautier's Leap. This architecture may be vernacular but it also had decidedly military strength. Danger was rife and the life of the abbey had to be protected at all costs.

Belle-Chaise

Above the Guardroom lay « Belle-Chaise », the Abbot's courtroom. It was here that he passed judgement, for he had the right to sentence anybody on his land.

Right : *Belle-Chaise.*
Below : *the abbey lodgings and the abbey seen from the south-east.*

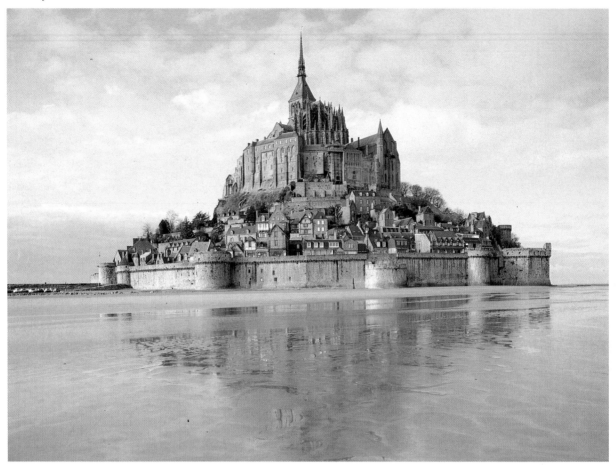

Above : *the town walls from the gates (on the left) to the Loop Tower (to the right).*

On previous pages : *the Guests' Chamber.*

Right : *the town seen from the chevet of the church.*

The only exceptions to this rule were criminal offences, for a man of the cloth was forbidden to spill blood. The Abbot sat on a throne, the chair or « chaise » which gave the chamber its name.

The town of Mont-Saint-Michel and its ramparts

The town

Mont Saint-Michel is also a « town » or, to be more precise, a small Norman village nestling at the foot of the abbey with which it has always been closely connected. The first houses were built on the north side ; later, they huddled on the south side. Pilgrims would then find inns and taverns awaiting them, just as today's visitors find hotels and restaurants. They bought badges of pilgrimage just as tourists buy souvenirs. A narrow street leads up to the monastery. A shortcut called the Chemin des Monteux was preferred by the locals, the Montois. A tiny church dedicated to St. Peter welcomes the faithful. A fine carving of the head of Christ, commissioned by André de Laure in 1483, is now kept in the sacristy. A small cemetery watched over by a granite Cross stands high above the sea close to the church. A few of the old houses have been preserved e.g. the 15th-century Hôtellerie de la Lycorne (the Unicorn Hostelry); others have been restored like the house said to have belonged to Tiphaine Raguenel, Du Guesclin's wife. Others have been built in a style considered to be appropriate.

The ramparts

In the 15th century, walls were erected right around the town. They were supported by towers, starting on the north side with its watchtower (a corbelled stone lookout post facing the shoreline) round to the town gates. There are obvious signs of progress when these towers are compared to the techniques used in earlier times, during the Middle Ages. In the meantime, the system of defence had become of vital im-

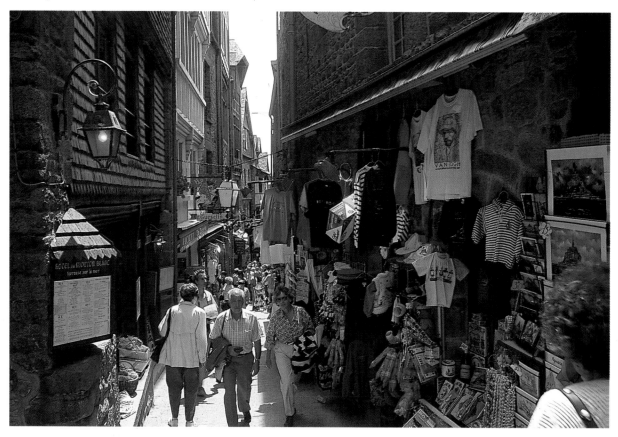

Above : *the main street in the village, the Grand-Rue.*

Opposite : *the « Mère Poulard ».*

portance. The towers were no longer miniature for-
tresses built to deal with minor local uprisings. Interconnected by a parapet walk, they no longer overloo-
ked the town walls ; on the contrary, it was the walls
that defended the towers. This is the principle behind
modern-day thinking viz « whatever provides the defence must itself be defended » (Germain Bazin). The
ramparts, with their numerous projections, run close
by the houses in the village, with machicolations at in-
tervals from which the defending forces could rain
projectiles down on the enemy. The Buckle Tower
was once known as a small bastion. It juts out over the
sand like a spur of rock and its shape is a forerunner
of the fortifications built by Vauban. The horizontal
slit windows were designed for bombards, the enormous late-mediaeval cannon. As a town surrounded
by walls was virtually impregnable, progress had been
made in artillery and methods of attack.

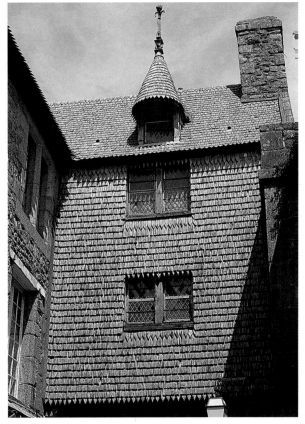

Above : *The parish church and graveyard.*
Below : *the Liberty Tower.*

The Artichoke House.
Overleaf : *the refectory.*

Above : *Robert Jolivet's coat-of-arms.*

Left, top : *the town walls.*

Left, bottom : *the half-moon battery or bastion, and the Buckle Tower.*

Opposite, top : *the North Tower.*

Opposite, bottom : *the hayloft and the Gabriel Tower.*

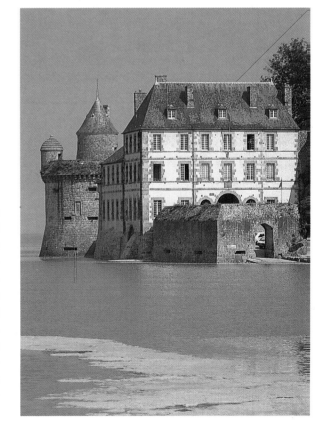

The Hayloft and the Gabriel tower (1524)

It was the king's lieutenant, Gabriel Dupuy, who completed the Mont's system of defence. And indeed at the beginning of the 16th century, the skill of the military engineer was almost at the peak of perfection, as is obvious from the Gabriel Tower. All possible angles of fire were catered for. The garrison could take action against any attack with all due speed. The cannon were set up inside the thick walls. The large bastion, which is reminiscent of the ones in Fougères Castle, defended the entrance to the hayloft. A chimney provided an outlet for the smoke. In the 17th century, a windmill was built on the platform.

Opposite : *Mont Saint-Michel as depicted in the Très Riches Heures du Duc de Berry (late 14th century).*

Photographic credits

Andia/F. Hamon : p.19. **Andia/E. Cattin :** p. 7. **A. Mauxion :** p. 5 t. **H. Boulé :** p. 55 t. **B. Dauleux :** p. 6 t, 28, 32, 45 t, 52, 58 b.

Wonderful Mont Saint-Michel

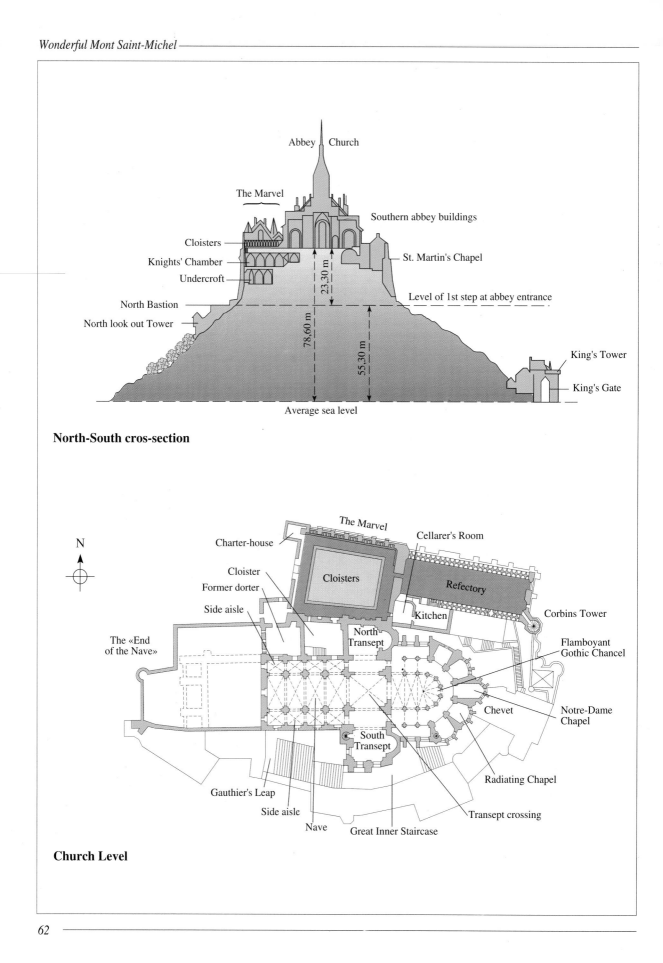

North-South cros-section

Abbey Church

The Marvel

Southern abbey buildings

Cloisters

Knights' Chamber

Undercroft

St. Martin's Chapel

North Bastion

North look out Tower

Level of 1st step at abbey entrance

King's Tower

King's Gate

23,30 m

78,60 m

55,30 m

Average sea level

Church Level

N

The Marvel

Charter-house

Cellarer's Room

Cloister

Former dorter

Cloisters

Refectory

Side aisle

Kitchen

Corbins Tower

The «End of the Nave»

North Transept

Flamboyant Gothic Chancel

Chevet

Notre-Dame Chapel

South Transept

Radiating Chapel

Gauthier's Leap

Side aisle

Nave

Great Inner Staircase

Transept crossing

The Marvel
Latrines
St. Mary Magdalen Chapel

Knights' Chamber

Guests' Chamber

Monks' Gallery

Corbins Tower
Crypt of the Mighty Pillars

Devil's dungeon

Crypt of the 30 Candles

Robert de Thorigny's apartments

Rock

Tank

Belle-Chaise

Perrine Tower

Our-Lady Underground

Bailiff's lodging

St. Stephen's Chapel

Hoist

Ossuary and wheel

St. Martin Crypt

Great Inner Staircase

Abbot's apartments

Intermediate level

The Marvel
Abbey walls
Plants, Gardens
Rock

The Marvel

Abbey Gardens

Undercroft

Almonry

Corbins Tower

Romanesque walk way

Aquilon

Barbican

Caretaker's lodge

Dungeons

Rock

The Marvel Courtyard

Forward Gate

Guard room

Perrine Tower

Great Inner Staircase

Site of Romanesque Hostel

Chapel of St. Catherine-of-the-Steps

Abbey apartments

Lower level

N

St. Aubert's
Spring

Claudine Tower

North Tower

St. Aubert's
Chapel

Guardroom

Buckle Tower

The Marvel

Minster

Half-moon
Battery

West
Terrace

St. Peter's
parish church

Abbey apartments

Foal Rise

Gabriel
Tower

Low Tower

Hayloft

*Seminar
Hall*

Hayloft Tower

Boulevard
Gate

Liberty Tower

Hayloft
Forework

P. O.

Burghers'
Guardroom
(Tourist Office)

Footbridge

Arcade Tower

Town Hall

Dyke

King's
Gate

King's
Tower

Forward
Gate

KEY TO SYMBOLS

- ☐ Entrance to town and abbey
- ☐ Open areas
- ▦ Rock
- ▦ Access to town walls
- ▦ Walls
- ▦ Plants, Gardens
- ☐ Buildings
- ▦ Abbey
- ▥ Steps

MAIN CHARACTERISTICS

- Length of dyke to Mont : 1 mile. • Circumference of Mont : 1/2 mile.
- Height of abbey above sea level : 255 ft.
- Size of Archangel : base to sword : 14 1/2 ft ; Archangel : 9 ft ; weight : almost 9 cwt.

Cet ouvrage a été imprimé par Aubin Imprimeur à Ligugé (86).
I.S.B.N. 2.7373.1126.8 - Dépôt légal : mars 1994
N° éditeur : 2455.02.09.03.94